MW01701188

Leaders Make Decisions

Dr. Tiana P. Clemons

Leaders Make Decisions

ISBN (Paperback): 978-0-9995734-9-5

Printed in the United States of America.
First edition, July 2025.

Published by Healed.Today Publishing, a trademarked imprint of Healed.Today™

For permissions, bulk orders, consulting, or speaking inquiries: info@tianapatrice.com

Dr. Tiana P. Clemons is a speaker, coach, and strategist who equips purpose-driven leaders to lead with emotional intelligence, wholeness, and clarity.

Her work has influenced executives, ministries, educators, and change-makers across the country.

This book is her invitation to lead differently...from the inside out.

About This Book

Leaders are defined by their decisions.

But what separates a good leader from a great one?

In *Leaders Make Decisions*, Dr. Tiana P. Clemons challenges leaders to dig beneath the surface of success and examine the emotional, spiritual, and mental clarity driving their choices.

Drawing from years of leadership, ministry, and executive coaching experience, she equips readers with the tools to confront fear, silence insecurity, and lead from a place of wisdom and wholeness.

This isn't just a leadership manual—it's a mirror, a compass, and a call to courage.

Whether you're leading a team, a classroom, a ministry, or a movement, you'll discover how to:

- Discern decisions with integrity and boldness
- Build a legacy rooted in emotional wholeness
- Navigate pressure without losing your purpose
- Lead others without abandoning yourself

Step into the kind of leadership that changes atmospheres and transforms lives...starting with your own.

Table of Contents

Author's Note

This book was born out of countless coaching sessions, boardroom conversations, late-night reflections, and moments where I had to face my own inner hesitations as a leader.

It's more than a book, it's a coaching experience if you allow it to be.

You'll notice that throughout these pages, I don't just share information, I ask you questions. I offer prompts. I slow you down on purpose. This is intentional. Because leadership isn't just about strategy. It's about soul. And far too often, leaders are trained to lead teams, but never trained to lead themselves.

So grab a pen. Highlight what hits. Pause when needed. Re-read if necessary. This book is written for the kind of leader who understands that growth doesn't happen in a rush…it happens in reflection.

You may also notice that *emotion*, *self-awareness*, and *wholeness* come up often. That's not by accident. Too many leadership books tell you what to do but not who to become. This one is different. Because your inner life *always* leaks into your outer leadership. So if this book feels personal, it's because leadership is personal.

You'll also see brief mentions of **faith** and **discernment** woven into the pages. Not in a preachy or religious way, but because I truly believe that great leadership is both practical and deeply grounded. Faith, for me, is a foundation and I won't pretend it doesn't influence the way I lead and coach. If you're someone who leads with conviction, you'll understand.

And finally, you might find parts of this book emotionally confronting. That's on purpose. I don't believe in surface-level development. I believe in transformation. And transformation isn't tidy…it's layered, slow, and sacred. But it's always worth it.

So let's begin this journey together. Not toward perfect leadership, but toward whole leadership.

Let's build something worth following from the inside out.

– Dr. Tiana

"

Every decision leaves a fingerprint.
Not just on results, but on people."

Introduction

Spoiler alert…This is not a leadership book about strategy.

It's not about influence, execution, or productivity. It's not about charisma, communication hacks, or how to scale your team. There are thousands of books that already do that, and many of them are brilliant.

But this book is different.

Leaders Make Decisions was born from my belief that leadership should begin where most books end: the soul of the leader. Because the truth is, we don't just lead from vision.

We lead from memory.

From belief.

From identity.

We lead from the parts of us that have been formed, and the parts that still need healing.

Most leadership models are built around external behavior: how to build high-performing teams, how to communicate better, how to execute under pressure. All valuable. All needed. But what's missing from that model is this: what's driving the leader beneath the strategy? That's where my leadership model comes in.

Because if the leader is unhealed, what good is the strategy? If the leader is leaking, the culture will reflect it. If the leader is unclear, the team will feel it. If the leader is reactive, the decision will suffer. And if the leader is insecure, the outcomes will never be enough.

What if leadership wasn't just about being the smartest in the room, but the most whole? What if decisions didn't have to come from ego or fear, but from alignment, identity, and wisdom? What if we taught leaders how to lead from healing, not just hustle?

That's what this book is about.

It's about redefining leadership through the lens of emotional wholeness, spiritual clarity, identity-rooted confidence, values-aligned decision-making, and courage birthed from healing…not pressure.

This book does not ignore execution, it just believes that execution without wholeness eventually collapses. It does not ignore structure, it just knows that structure built on insecurity becomes control. And it does not ignore influence, but it insists that influence is dangerous when it flows from a fractured soul.

If you're tired of leading from pressure...If you're successful but secretly burned out... If you've mastered leadership skills but struggle with the voice in your head... If you long to lead from a deeper place, this book is for you.

Because the greatest leaders don't just make smart decisions. They make sound ones. Emotionally sound. Spiritually grounded. Courageously clear.

And that kind of leadership? It doesn't just build businesses. It heals cultures. It restores trust. It transforms people.

So let's get to the root.

Let's uncover what's been buried beneath performance. Let's confront what we've been taught to avoid. Let's give language to the unspoken, space to the internal, and strength to the soul of how we lead.

Let's make decisions from a different place. Because at the end of the day, Leaders Make Decisions..but whole leaders make the ones that matter most.

PART I

The Inner Life of Leadership

“

The most dangerous leaders aren't the loud ones or even the wrong ones, they're the ones leading from unhealed places with unchecked influence.”

CHAPTER 1

The Weight of Leadership

Leadership is weighty. The moment a leader walks into a room, something shifts. Whether it's a CEO stepping into a board meeting, a principal greeting their staff, or a team lead showing up for a project check-in, their presence carries an invisible weight. That weight is the sum total of influence, decisions, expectations, and the unseen emotional energy that leadership demands.

But here's the truth: leadership doesn't begin when others start following. It begins in the unseen places before the meeting, before the strategy session, before the platform. It begins inside the leader, and it flows out of everything the leader has access to.

Too often, leadership is framed as a title or a tier of power. And if we're honest, leadership is too often pursued for the allure of the title or the perceived power it holds. But real leadership is not about having a seat at the table; it's about who you are at the table. It's about what overflows from your inner life: your values, your emotional intelligence, your ability to discern, your courage to confront, and your willingness to grow. It's about what shows when you are triggered, and what's revealed when stakes are high.

Whether you realize it or not, every decision you make as a leader is a reflection of your internal world. It reveals your clarity or confusion. Your confidence or your fear. Your healing or your hidden wounds. Because the external influence of a leader is only as stable as what's happening behind the scenes, in the heart, the mind, the history.

These are the leadership conversations that rarely make it into the boardroom or the pulpit. The ones that don't get posted on LinkedIn. The ones we gloss over with the right buzzwords and the perfect suit or skirt. But they matter. In fact, they may matter more than anything else.

Can we talk about the parts of leadership most people avoid? The weight no one wants to carry aloud. The fear of getting it wrong and being found out. The pressure to be the answer for everyone else while secretly wondering who sees you. The emotional exhaustion that doesn't show up in your resume but lives in your body. The desire to do it differently, but the silence that surrounds anything that sounds too "soft."

We've been taught that emotions are a liability in leadership. That feeling too deeply disqualifies you from leading powerfully. But what if the opposite is true? What if the leaders who are willing to feel are actually the ones most equipped to heal what's broken in their teams, classrooms, churches, or companies?

Emotional wholeness is not weakness. It's wisdom. It's not soft. It's strategic. It's not a side conversation. It's the center of courageous, sustainable, and transformative leadership.

The Responsibility of Decision-Making

Every leader must learn to carry the responsibility of decision-making, and not just for the sake of outcomes, but for the process itself.

For example, imagine a school principal deciding whether to expel a student who has repeatedly broken the rules. On paper, the data says removal is justified. But a leader rooted in wholeness asks deeper questions: What's going on beneath this student's behavior? What does justice look like alongside compassion? How will this decision shape not just the student's future, but the culture of the school moving forward?

The outcome matters, but so does the process: Who was consulted? Was it done with integrity? Was it driven by fear or alignment?

That's what sets whole leaders apart. They don't just rush toward results. They walk through the process with clarity, conviction, and care.

Decisions are not made in a vacuum. They ripple outward, touching teams, families, clients, and cultures. In fact, most decisions a leader makes don't just affect the task at hand; they subtly shape the culture of an organization, the morale of a team, and the trajectory of people's lives.

The Impact of Decisions on Others

Let's be honest, leaders don't just make decisions for themselves. They make decisions that shape the climate of entire rooms. We've all experienced it: a leader walks in and suddenly the room is filled with energy and excitement, fueling growth, motivation, and perseverance. And we've experienced the opposite too, a leader whose presence drains the atmosphere, silences ideas, and tightens everyone's posture.

Pause for a moment and recall one of those moments. How did you feel in your body? What thoughts ran through your mind? How did it impact your energy, your creativity, your effort afterward? Now, ask yourself honestly: Which kind of leader are you?

Because leadership isn't just about what you say. It's about the atmosphere you carry. And every decision you make contributes to the atmosphere, for better or for worse.

Leadership Isn't About a Title

At some point in their journey, every impactful leader must confront a personal truth: leadership is not who they are, it's how they live. For some reason, we've confused influence with visibility. True leadership is not platform-dependent. It is presence-dependent. It is not loud or showy. It is often quiet, consistent, and deeply rooted.

A title does not grant permission to lead. Integrity does. Character does. Consistency does. The overflow of the inner life is what qualifies a leader, not the business card or the seat at the head of the table.

When Wholeness Shapes Decisions

There's a difference between making a decision and making a whole decision. A whole decision isn't just correct on paper; it's aligned with your values, your identity, and your emotional intelligence. Whole decisions may not always feel good in the moment or earn the popular vote, but they reflect maturity, not manipulation.

Whole decisions are clear, grounded, and intentional.

Self-Leadership Precedes Organizational Leadership

Before you can lead others well, you must first lead yourself. That doesn't mean you have to have it all together, but it does mean you must be willing to go first. Wholeness isn't about perfection. It's about intentionality. It's about self-awareness.

Transformational Leadership in Action

William is the COO of a mid-sized tech company. Known for his sharp strategic mind, he is often relied upon for fast decisions and flawless execution. But behind the scenes, William struggled with imposter syndrome. For years, he overcompensated by overworking, micromanaging his teams, and avoiding feedback.

After attending a leadership development retreat focused on emotional intelligence, William began doing the inner work. He started therapy. He invited his executive coach to help him identify blind spots. Within months, his team noted a change: more collaboration, more psychological safety, and a noticeable rise in morale.

A New Model of Leadership

We've inherited leadership models that prioritized metrics over people, control over collaboration, and perfection over presence. But that model is crumbling. And rightly so.

In its place, a new model is rising: leadership that flows from the inside out. Leadership that starts with the soul. Leadership that says: I've done the inner work. I know who I am. And because I know who I am, I know how to lead you.

🖊 Leadership Audit: What's Pouring Out of You?

Ask yourself:

- What is truly driving my decisions right now: fear, pressure, ego, or clarity?
- When was the last time I made a hard decision and felt peace instead of panic?
- What emotions tend to hijack my leadership? Anger, anxiety, control, insecurity?
- Have I confused my title with my identity?

Because from this day forward, you don't just lead with power. You lead with wholeness.

The world does not need more burnt-out, image-conscious leaders who know how to put on a show. It certainly doesn't need ego-driven, title-seeking performers parading as visionaries. What the world needs are leaders whose inner lives are strong enough to carry the weight of outer influence. Leaders who understand that their character must run deeper than their charisma. That true leadership isn't about spotlight, applause, or control, it's about service, stewardship, and substance. A leader who understands that influence without integrity is dangerous. That gifting without grounding is reckless. And that the work within is just as sacred as the work they're called to do out loud.

Howard Thurman, a civil rights leader and theologian, said: "Don't ask what the world needs. Ask what makes you come alive, and go do it. Because what the world needs is people who have come alive."

A leader who has come alive through healing, wholeness, and emotional growth is unstoppable. They don't just lead, they shift atmospheres. They don't just manage, they inspire. They don't just decide, they discern. So, leader, what have you discerned about your own leadership? And what kind of atmosphere are you creating, intentionally or unintentionally, every time you enter the room?

Chapter 1 Key Takeaways:

- Leadership is what overflows from the inner life, not what's written on a business card.
- Every decision made by a leader has a ripple effect on culture, teams, and people.
- Fear, if unexamined, becomes the silent driver behind indecision and dysfunction.
- Whole leadership is emotionally aware, rooted in values, and free from the pressure to prove.
- The future of leadership is not louder, it's deeper.

As we move into the next chapter, we'll explore how emotional intelligence becomes the foundation for sound leadership, and how knowing yourself allows you to lead others well. But before we go there, take this truth with you: You are not responsible for having all the answers. You are responsible for stewarding the weight of leadership with honesty, healing, and courage. Because from this day forward, you don't just lead with power, you lead with wholeness.

“

Self-awareness is not a soft skill. It’s a non-negotiable.”

CHAPTER 2

The Emotional Intelligence Factor

Before any strategic move, before any confident "yes" or courageous "no," there is a moment of silence, a pause where self-awareness is either present or absent. That pause is what separates a reactive leader from a grounded one. It's also where emotional intelligence starts. Leadership is not simply about what you do, it's about who you are while doing it. The best decisions don't come from having all the information. They come from knowing who you are, what you believe, what you feel, and what truly matters in the moment.

So, let's pause here and assess: Who are you?

Who are you when no one is watching?
Who are you behind closed doors, with your parents, your children, your friends?
Who are you to your spouse?
But most importantly...who are you to yourself?

This is where true leadership begins, not in a title, but in truth. And studies show that leaders with higher emotional intelligence make faster, more effective decisions and experience significantly less burnout. They aren't just efficient; they're aligned.

Self-Awareness as the Foundation for Sound Decisions

My uncle is a 70-year-old, self-taught home builder. I grew up watching him pour sweat and tears into every project, inspecting each detail with painstaking care. I watched workers come and go, but I noticed that only a few stayed.

As a young leader in training, I remember one thing he told me that stuck:
"I can only build with people who understand the process, and who respect the journey ahead."

You see, when you're pouring the foundation of a house, there's no room for error. One miscalculation and you risk everything, starting over, wasted materials, or worse, a home built on uneven ground.

A home on uneven ground.
That sentence still lingers with me.

I carry it with me when I coach leaders across industries, because if leadership is a house, then self-awareness is the foundation. You can stack vision, strategy, and execution on top, but without self-awareness, and the grounded confidence it brings your leadership won't hold. Not under pressure. Not over time.

Self-awareness is the ability to recognize your own thoughts, emotions, biases, and patterns in real time.

(Let's pause there for just a moment.)

Many leaders believe they're self-aware...until an iceberg hits their boat. Real-time self-awareness means knowing when you're being triggered, when your ego is taking the lead, when fear is whispering in your ear, and when old wounds are shaping present reactions. It's the courage to pause and respond wisely instead of reacting impulsively.Without this awareness, decisions are made in the fog, choices that might look good on paper but feel off in spirit. And that kind of decision-making is dangerous. Self-awareness is not a soft skill. It's a non-negotiable for leaders who want to lead with integrity, impact, and wholeness.

Daniel Goleman, the pioneer of emotional intelligence, puts it like this: "If you are tuned out of your own emotions, you will be poor at reading them in other people."And if you can't read the emotions of others, you'll consistently misread the room, misjudge your team's needs, and misstep in critical moments. This isn't just a leadership gap, it's a leadership liability. Poor emotional awareness leads to poor leadership, and poor leadership always leads to poor results.

Self-aware leaders ask questions like:

- What am I really feeling right now?
- Why did that situation frustrate me so much?
- Am I leading from fear, or from alignment?
- What story am I telling myself, and is it true?

When you skip those questions, you lead reactively. You act from assumption. You rely on instinct when what's needed is insight. But when you lead from a place of awareness, you make decisions that are not just logical, they are whole.

Regulating Emotions to Avoid Reactionary Choices

Now, let's be honest, leadership doesn't always give you time to process. Emails come in fast. Teams want answers now. Board members have expectations. Deadlines quickly become today-lines. And all of this may be happening faster than your brain can keep up. Here's what you need to know: there is a difference between *leading in* urgent situations and *leading from* urgency. Leading from urgency is dangerous. It's an anxious posture that often gets leaders in trouble. You might make the decision fast, but not well. That's why self-awareness and emotional regulation are essential.

Let's address the elephant in the room: self-awareness and emotional regulation are not signs of weak leadership. In fact, they're the only way your leadership can be strong, grounded, and aligned. Regulating emotions doesn't mean suppressing them. It's not about being stoic or cold. It's about being able to feel fully without being ruled blindly.

(Yes, you should probably highlight that, and make it your new affirmation.)

Emotional regulation means creating an internal pause, so the emotion doesn't speak louder than your wisdom. A regulated leader can feel the pressure of the room and still remain centered. They can experience frustration but respond with clarity. They can acknowledge anxiety and still act in alignment with their values. This is the kind of leader we should all aspire to be.

Let's make this practical and remember to be honest. This book isn't about fixing others. It's about you putting on your own mask first.

- When you're feeling overwhelmed, do you retreat, lash out, or pause?
- When someone challenges your idea, do you get defensive or curious?
- When conflict arises, do you internalize or initiate healthy confrontation?

The way you handle those moments says more about your leadership than any credential or résumé. This book is not about *if* emotional waves will come, it's about WHEN they come, *how* you ride them.

Repeat after me: Emotionally reactive leaders erode trust. Regulated leaders build safety.

Safety is what gives teams permission to take risks, share ideas, and stay engaged. As a leader, your emotional tone becomes the thermostat for the entire team. It sets the climate, whether people feel free to speak, safe to fail, or pressured to perform. So let's pause and assess: based on where you are right now, what's the temperature you're setting? Is your thermostat warm: engaging, trusting, and collaborative? Or is it cold: marked by fear, silence, and disconnection?

According to TalentSmart, emotional intelligence accounts for nearly 58% of a leader's job performance, and 90% of top performers have high EQ.

Do you understand why wholeness is not optional? If your emotional landscape is unhealed, you will project your unprocessed wounds onto your people. But when you've done the work, when you've regulated your own emotions, you create a space for others to do the same.

We must learn to recognize the space between the trigger and our response, because in that pause lies the power to choose wisely. That space is what emotionally intelligent leaders cultivate. They expand the gap between what happens and how they respond. And in that gap, better decisions are made.

Empathy and Its Role in Effective Leadership

Remember the elephant in the room? Let's address it again. Empathy is often mistaken for weakness. But in reality, it is one of the most courageous forms of leadership. To empathize is to enter into someone else's emotional world without trying to fix, avoid, or outperform it. It is the capacity to hold space for both your perspective and theirs, even when they conflict. For leaders, empathy is not just a "nice to have", it's a *strategic advantage.* Why? Because decisions made without empathy are decisions made in isolation. You may hit your KPIs, goals and agenda, and still lose your people. You may win the quarter and still lose the trust. You may push out the product and still create burnout. Empathy is the difference between transactional leadership and transformational leadership. Transactional leadership says, "I care about your output." Transformational leadership says, "I care about *you*."

Simon Sinek describes this as the essence of great leadership: "Leadership is not about being in charge. It's about taking care of those in your charge."

Empathy enhances every leadership skill:

- It makes your communication clearer, because you consider how it lands.
- It makes your feedback more impactful, because you tailor it to how someone receives truth.
- It makes your meetings more productive, because you notice when something unspoken is holding people back.

But perhaps most importantly, empathy builds emotional safety. When people feel emotionally safe, they innovate. They take risks. They speak up. They trust their instincts. And that doesn't happen by accident, it happens by intentional leadership design.

A leader without empathy will often say things like:

- "I just don't understand why they're so sensitive."
- "They need to leave their personal life at the door."
- "This is business, not therapy."

But those statements betray a deep misunderstanding of how people, and performance, actually work. Repeat after me: Empathy is not emotional coddling. It's emotional intelligence in motion. It allows you to lead from a place of connection instead of control And when empathy guides your decisions, people feel seen. When people feel seen, they show up fully. And when they show up fully, success is realized, movements gain momentum, and vision becomes reality.

Healing Emotional Wounds to Lead with Clarity and Compassion

So what does this mean for you? The reality is, you cannot lead others from a place of wholeness if you haven't gone there yourself. One of the most overlooked areas of leadership development is *healing*. Not coaching. Not skill-building. Not networking. But healing. Many leaders are making high-level decisions while carrying childhood wounds. They're negotiating million-dollar deals while still seeking approval from a father who never affirmed them. They're managing teams while harboring unspoken resentment toward past betrayals. And all of it leaks into their leadership.

Unhealed wounds show up in subtle ways:

- Over-apologizing for setting boundaries.
- Avoiding conflict to maintain surface-level peace.
- Micromanaging because you don't trust others.
- Shutting down emotionally during moments of vulnerability.

Healing allows leaders to stop leading from survival mode. It frees them from the burden of performing for validation. It softens the defensiveness that once felt necessary. And it gives them back their voice, not the loud one, but the rooted one. The sound voice. Firmly planted.

Brené Brown said it this way: "You either walk inside your story and own it, or you stand outside your story and hustle for your worthiness."

When a leader does the healing work, their decisions start coming from wholeness instead of woundedness. They don't just lead well, they lead with *clarity* and *compassion.* Clarity because their inner noise is quieter. They can discern what matters most. They can move with less second-guessing and more conviction. Compassion because they remember what it feels like to be human. To struggle. To overcome. They don't weaponize their title, they steward it. Yes, leadership is stewardship.

Think of it this way: a healed leader is a *safe leader.* And safety is what allows people to bring their full selves to the table.

Becoming an Emotionally Intelligent Leader

Like many leaders, maybe you've taken countless leadership and IQ tests. And while the results might be free, the transformation will cost you. Emotional intelligence isn't developed in a workshop and perfected overnight. It's cultivated over time, through intention, reflection, and hard-won growth.It is formed in the fires of lived experience, honest self-reflection, and intentional growth. The good news? It's learnable. The hard truth? It requires humility.

Leaders who develop emotional intelligence consistently practice:

- **Pause before reacting.** They ask, "What am I really feeling? What's driving this reaction?"

- **Name the emotion.** They identify it ("I feel overwhelmed," "I feel overlooked") so it doesn't hijack their judgment.
- **Choose alignment over impulse.** They filter responses through values, not moods.
- **Lean in with curiosity.** Especially when they feel challenged. They ask, "Help me understand," rather than assuming intent.
- **Do the inner work.** They engage in therapy, coaching, prayer, journaling, and other practices that allow them to confront what's unresolved.

Emotional intelligence is not about getting soft, it's about getting sharp. Clear. Anchored. It allows leaders to navigate conflict without causing trauma, to deliver truth without shame, and to challenge people without crushing them. When EQ is high, fear is low. And when fear is low, trust grows. And where there's trust, there's transformation.

🖋 Leadership Audit: Where Are You Now?

Take 10 minutes to audit your current emotional intelligence as a leader. Reflect honestly on the following questions:

Self-Awareness

- Do I know what I'm feeling in real time, or only after the fact?
- How often do I pause to reflect on what's driving my decisions?
- Can I articulate my values and use them to guide my leadership?

Emotional Regulation

- When triggered, do I pause or react?
- How do I respond under pressure—with calm or with control?

- Do others feel emotionally safe around me, even when we disagree?

Empathy

- Do I genuinely try to understand others' perspectives, even when I don't agree?
- Can I hold space for someone else's emotions without needing to fix them?
- Do people on my team feel seen, heard, and valued?

Healing & Wholeness

- What unresolved wounds may be influencing how I lead?
- Am I leading from identity or insecurity?
- What intentional steps am I taking to heal and grow emotionally?

After reviewing your responses, identify 1–2 areas where you feel strong, and 1–2 areas that need more intentional development. You don't need to be perfect, you just need to be aware and willing.

Remember, leadership isn't about removing emotion from your decision-making. It's about learning how to understand it, manage it, and integrate it with wisdom. Emotionally intelligent leaders are not perfect, but they are present. They make decisions that don't just move projects forward; they move people forward.

Because ultimately, the best decisions aren't just the smartest ones, they're the most *whole* ones.

Chapter 2 Takeaways: The Emotional Intelligence Factor

1. Self-awareness is the starting point of sound decision-making. Without it, leaders react rather than respond.
2. Emotionally intelligent leaders regulate their emotions, creating space between stimulus and response.
3. Empathy is a strategic advantage, not a liability. It builds trust, psychological safety, and team cohesion.
4. Healing is a leadership discipline. Unhealed wounds distort judgment. Wholeness clarifies it.
5. Emotional intelligence can be learned, but it requires intentionality, feedback, and courage.
6. What's happening in your inner life always shows up in your leadership. Always.

“We call it leadership, but it's often self-protection wearing a blazer.”

CHAPTER 3

Whole and Healthy Decision-Making

Imagine this, a senior executive stands in front of her leadership team, facing one of the hardest decisions of her career. The company she runs will have to either downsize or pivot the business model entirely, both options come with massive implications. She has all the data, financial forecasts, and industry trends at her fingertips. Logically, the pivot makes sense. It is bold, future-oriented, and filled with risk. Emotionally, she felt the strain of uncertainty and the weight of her team's livelihood.

Before making the final decision, she didn't sit in a boardroom crunching more numbers. Instead, she went home, sat in silence, and asked herself the question most leaders are never trained to ask: *What's actually driving me right now, fear or clarity? Am I making this decision to preserve something or to lead forward?*

This is the heartbeat of whole and healthy decision-making: not just what we choose, but what's driving the choice.

The Intersection of Logic and Emotion

We've often been taught to compartmentalize in leadership, to place logic on one side of the table and emotion on the other, as if the two cannot coexist. This kind of training produced leaders who are well-versed in systems and strategy, but emotionally illiterate and incapable of leading beyond the walls of logic. Transformational leadership, however, requires more. It happens at the intersection of logic and emotion where decisions are both sound and human, and where cultures shift because people feel both seen and guided.

Logic gives us strategy. Emotion gives it meaning.

When leaders rely solely on logic, they risk becoming cold, mechanical, and disconnected from the human realities of leadership. When they rely solely on emotion, they risk becoming reactive, ungrounded, and inconsistent. But when the two work together, when emotional intelligence fuels strategic thinking, leaders become both effective, trustworthy and unstoppable.

Think of a leader trying to decide whether to keep a struggling department or cut it for efficiency. The logical answer might point to financial downsizing, while the emotional reality points to team morale, long-term trust, and the personal stories attached to those positions. A whole and healthy leader doesn't ignore either voice. Instead, they create space for both to be heard. They slow down long enough to evaluate what the numbers reveal *and* what the decision may cost relationally. They ask the hard questions: Even if the data calls for a cut, can the organization sustain, thrive, and grow through the relational aftermath? They weigh the impact not just in terms of profit, but in trust, morale, and long-term culture.

It's not about making soft decisions, it's about making *whole* ones. Because people don't just remember *what* you decided; they remember *how* you made them feel when you decided it.

Core Values as a Compass

When leaders are uncertain, the temptation is to chase certainty, to look for the safest bet, the most widely accepted answer, the most defendable outcome. As humans, we often associate certainty with peace, because it gives the illusion of control. But in leadership, certainty is often a moving target. It shifts with the data, the people, the moment. Instead of chasing it, wise leaders anchor themselves in something steadier, something that doesn't waver with changing circumstances.

That's where core values come in.

When I train executive teams, I often begin with vision casting. It sounds simple, but it's where most organizations begin to drift. In this process, we unpack not just casting vision, but adopting culture and anchoring values. Because core values aren't wall art. They aren't buzzwords tucked into strategic plans or recited at board meetings to check a box. They are internal anchors, truths we return to when we're unsure of what to do. Leaders who make consistent, healthy decisions often have this in common: they know their values, and they don't negotiate them in moments of pressure.

Let's say one of your values is *honor.* That value will shape how you handle conflict, how you give feedback, how you exit people from your team. It means you don't ghost people. You don't gossip behind closed doors. You don't make reactive decisions that violate the dignity of the people you lead even when you're frustrated. If your value is *courage*, you don't let fear dictate silence in meetings where hard truth needs to be spoken. If your value is *excellence*, you don't settle for mediocrity because you're tired or under deadline. But here's the thing: values only work as a compass if we're *honest* about them and if we revisit them often. Some of us are making decisions based on values that were handed to us, not chosen by us.

I wish I could write that a hundred times if it meant you would truly receive it.

A former boss's leadership style. A parent's voice in your head. A culture's unspoken expectations. These borrowed values often shape our leadership before we've had a chance to question them. And if we're not careful, they can lead us into roles, relationships, and decisions that betray who we truly are.

So let me ask you: are your values borrowed...or are they anchored?

Whole leaders take the time to ask:

- What do I truly believe matters most?
- What am I willing to lose to stay aligned with that belief?
- What value must remain non-negotiable in every decision I make?

This kind of clarity becomes liberating. You stop over-explaining your decisions. You stop second-guessing your instincts. You stop leading for applause. You start leading from alignment. And one day, you'll look up and realize...you are finally, firmly planted, standing as the leader you were always meant to be.

The Role of Faith, Discernment, and Wisdom

Not every decision can be made with a spreadsheet. In fact, some of the most powerful decisions you'll ever make as a leader won't come from a strategy session, they'll come from stillness. From that quiet inner voice, the nudge, the check in your spirit that says, *This is the way, go in it.*

This is where faith and wisdom come in.

We don't talk about it enough in leadership, especially in corporate spaces. But by now, you probably know this about me: I'm not the kind of leader who can ignore or avoid it. Faith is foundational. It grounds everything I do and deeply informs how I grow and guide other leaders. For leaders who operate from a place of wholeness, faith and discernment aren't weird or mystical. They are necessary. They are sacred tools, anchors in uncertainty, compasses in chaos. And when used with wisdom, they help leaders know not just *what* to do, but *when* and *how* to move with conviction.

Faith reminds us that leadership is not about control. It's about stewardship. You are not responsible for *everything*. You are responsible for *your obedience*. You are responsible for listening, discerning, and trusting that sometimes the best move isn't the most popular, it's the most obedient. Discernment is not guessing. It's informed instinct. It's the product of lived experience, spiritual awareness, and deep listening. It's why an aware leader might walk into a room and say, *Something's off, we need to pause before we push this forward.* And they end up preventing a major cultural misstep.

Wisdom, then, is the integration of all three: logic, emotion, and spirit. It is not just about *what* is right, it is about *when* and *how* it is right.

A wise leader asks:

- Is this the right move?
- Is this the right *time* for the move?
- And is this the right *way* to make the move?

Wisdom slows us down. It listens before speaking. It seeks counsel. It considers legacy over urgency. And it often whispers when everything else is shouting.

Leading Beneath The Surface

Leadership decisions are fruit. They are what others see. They're discussed in meetings, announced in memos, evaluated on performance reviews. But long before a decision is made, a seed has been planted. That seed is internal, it's your identity, your story, your unspoken fears, and your longings for affirmation or safety.

We talk a lot about outcomes in leadership. But what if we paid just as much attention to the *origins*? Where did the decision start? A leader may pride themselves on being decisive. But underneath that drive could be a fear of looking incompetent. Another may seem collaborative but may actually be avoiding confrontation due to past rejection. We call it leadership, but it's often self-protection wearing a blazer. That's why whole and healthy leadership requires us to go deeper than our decision trees. We need to ask: *What is this decision revealing about me?* What old script is playing in the background of my thinking? What part of my identity is being tested here?

Character isn't tested in easy decisions, it's tested when everything in you wants to self-protect, but you choose to show up with integrity anyway.

Coaching in Real Time

One executive I coached was struggling to let go of a toxic high-performer. She knew keeping this person was hurting team morale and compromising values, but something kept her stuck. In one session, she finally named it: "I'm afraid of looking like I failed in hiring them." Boom. Now we could make some strategic progress.

It wasn't just a performance issue. It was a personal one. Her identity was wrapped in her ability to not only lead well, but hire well. Her sense of being a capable leader was tied to the decision she made months ago. Letting the employee go felt like admitting she had been wrong. And if she was wrong, it triggered the deeper belief that she had failed…again. Once she addressed the root,the need to prove she was always right, she was able to make the hard, healthy call without shame.

This is what whole leadership looks like. Not just managing the visible fruit, but digging up the hidden roots. Making healthy decisions doesn't mean you'll always choose the easiest path. In fact, it often means doing what's right even when it costs more. But there's a deep peace that comes from knowing your decision wasn't made from fear, pressure, or the need to perform, it was made from wholeness.

And that kind of decision? It multiplies.

It builds trust. It strengthens culture. It models something different for the people watching. Because at the end of the day, leadership isn't just about what you build, it's about what you leave behind in others.

When you lead from the inside out, the decisions you make don't just impact systems. They impact souls. Those souls influence homes. Those homes shape communities. And those communities become the backbone of generational legacy. All because one leader decided to lead from a whole place.

🖊 The Wholeness Audit: Leading from Identity, Not Insecurity

Take a few quiet moments to reflect on these prompts. Let them guide you deeper into self-awareness:

1. When I make decisions, what am I most afraid of? (Looking weak? Being rejected? Losing control?)
2. What values am I most proud of living by? Where do I still struggle to embody them consistently?
3. Do I know the difference between my *true voice* and the voice of my fear?
4. Are there any past wounds influencing how I handle authority, trust, or conflict?
5. When I made my last major decision, what was the emotion underneath it?
6. What does leading from a *healed place* look like for me?
7. How often do I invite faith, discernment and wisdom into my decision-making?

These aren't checklist items. They're soul check-ins. And the more you lead from this space, the less you'll need to perform leadership, and the more you'll simply *be* a leader.

Chapter 3 Takeaways: Whole and Healthy Decision-Making

- Healthy leadership lives at the intersection of logic and emotion. You need both strategy and soul to lead with balance.
- Core values are your compass. Without them, your decisions will sway with the winds of pressure and performance.
- Faith, discernment, and wisdom matter. Whole leaders don't just follow what's trending they follow what's true and timely.
- The real work of decision-making starts beneath the surface. Your character, story, and healing shape everything you lead.
- Lead from identity, not insecurity. You don't need to prove your leadership when you're rooted in who you are.

PART II

From Reaction to Responsibility

"

There's a particular kind of exhaustion that comes from almost deciding."

CHAPTER 4

Overcoming Decision Paralysis

There's a particular kind of exhaustion that comes from almost deciding. It's the fatigue of the leader who's stayed up too many nights rehearsing the same scenarios. The one who has created three versions of the same email draft but can't bring themselves to hit send. The one who spends more time circling a choice than actually making one.

Does any of this sound familiar?

A Harvard Business Review study shows that people make up to 35,000 decisions a day and leadership decisions account for the most energy-draining. This could lead to decision paralysis. And it is one of the most costly, hidden threats to impactful leadership. At first glance, it doesn't look like failure.

It looks like responsibility.
Thoroughness.
Wisdom.

But in reality, it's a slow drain of clarity and courage. It's the silent thief of momentum. And left unchecked, it leaves leaders stuck in cycles of inaction, second-guessing, and self-doubt.

It's easy to assume that indecision only stems from a lack of knowledge. But more often, indecision stems from fear. Fear of being wrong. Fear of disappointing others. Fear of failing. Fear of being judged. I like to call this space the "in between." In between good and great.

In between success and failure. In between clarity and confusion. In between the urge to lead and the fear of being exposed. These fears, if left unexamined, become the silent rulers of a leader's choices. And, if you haven't learned by now, fear-led decisions rarely serve anyone well.

John C. Maxwell once said, "A leader is one who knows the way, goes the way, and shows the way." But what happens when fear clouds the way? What happens when the greatest distractions aren't the things around you…but the fear within you?

Decision paralysis is rarely about the decision itself, it's about what the decision represents. For many leaders, the fear isn't just, "What if I make the wrong call?" It's deeper: "What will they think of me if I fail?" "Will I still be trusted?" "Will I still belong?"

It's less about the task and more about identity. This isn't just a theory. It's a lived conversation. This comes from years of hundreds of conversations with leaders surrounding their indecision—leaders in education, government agencies, and entrepreneurship. Leaders in corporate settings and ministry spaces. Leaders in and out of the workplace or simply leaders within their homes and community environments. The root of their indecision almost always traced back to fear, fear attacking something they valued deeply enough to create internal paralysis.

These fears aren't always irrational. They often stem from past experiences, such as leaders who were punished for taking bold risks, overlooked for promotions, or who watched other leaders crash and burn under pressure. Moments that should have been moments of healthy navigation created fear-based leaders with leaky leadership. The trauma of watching failure, or living it, can calcify into hesitation. And hesitation, in the wrong moments, becomes a form of silent sabotage.

Fear of criticism is a particularly dangerous snare. Leaders under the weight of others' opinions will constantly shape-shift, saying yes when they mean no, and remaining silent when their voice is needed most. They will over-apologize to avoid conflict or over-control to avoid being questioned.

Here's the truth: no leader escapes criticism. Theodore Roosevelt put it best when he said: "It is not the critic who counts; not the man who points out how the strong man stumbles… The credit belongs to the man who is actually in the arena."

Leadership is not for the faint of heart. But the answer to fear is not false courage or manufactured confidence. It's emotional healing and inner truth. When a leader heals from the fears that once dictated their actions, they become dangerous, not in a harmful way, but in a holy one.

Dangerous to complacency.

Dangerous to dysfunction.

Dangerous to the systems that thrive on silence and comfort.

Wholeness makes a leader unshakeable. And an unshakeable, fortified, firmly planted leader is one that will change the world.

To overcome decision paralysis, we have to confront what's really happening underneath the hesitation. Remember, the fruit starts with the root. Because no leader can lead forward while stuck in limbo.

Risk vs. Reward: The Hidden Equation

The reality is every decision carries a cost. And decisions have to be made. That's leadership.

But not every decision carries equal weight. Part of overcoming paralysis is learning how to appropriately weigh the risks and rewards and not allowing your wounds or issues to inflate them. Leaders often get stuck when every decision feels like life or death.

Should you restructure the team? Launch a new program? End a partnership? Your mind can start spinning through dozens of scenarios, each one ending in either triumph or disaster.

Here's the shift: healthy leaders stop catastrophizing every possible outcome. They recognize that risk does not always equal loss, and reward is not always immediate.

Go ahead and say it with me: Risk does not always equal loss, and reward is not always immediate.

A whole leader knows how to step back and ask:

- What is the actual risk here, not just the one my fear is imagining?
- What happens if I don't decide? What will that cost over time?
- If this fails, will it be fatal or simply a learning curve?
- What new doors might open on the other side of this decision?

Let's take an example: a department lead is considering removing a long-standing policy that no longer serves the team. Logically, the data says it's time. Emotionally, there's fear: "This has always been our way. Will I offend the original creators? Will people resist me?"

Without the ability to properly assess risk versus reward, the leader will stay stuck in hypothetical scenarios, letting imagined backlash outweigh real progress. When we linger too long in the "what ifs," we miss the possibility of "what could be." And what could be… might just be extraordinary.

Pivot or Persevere?

There's a moment in every leader's journey where the question isn't "what to do" but when to let go. Is it time to pivot? Or press through?

This can apply to a relationship, a strategy, a goal, or even a vision you've nurtured for years. Sometimes, what started in vision becomes a trap when we don't make room for redirection.

Pivoting isn't quitting. It's discerning. But many leaders feel shame even thinking about changing course, as if doing so signals weakness or inconsistency.

The truth? Some of the wisest leaders are the ones who had the courage to reroute when the path changed beneath their feet. Persevering isn't always brave. Sometimes, it's just familiar. And familiarity can feel like faithfulness, but in reality, it may be fear of starting over.

Here are a few heart-check questions for these moments:

- Am I holding on because I still believe in the vision or because I'm afraid to face the unknown?
- Is this resistance a sign to grow stronger, or an invitation to surrender?
- If I remove my ego, what would wisdom tell me to do?

The Spiral of Overthinking

Overthinking is one of leadership's most polished liabilities. On the outside, it looks like diligence. Internally, it feels like torment. A torment that no one else sees.

You run through every scenario, talk to five people, read ten books, write three pros and cons lists and still feel unsure.

At its root, overthinking is usually about control. If I analyze enough, I can prevent pain. If I prepare thoroughly enough, I can avoid failure.

But what if I told you that's a false sense of confidence, one that quietly fuels a cycle destined to end in the very failure you were trying to avoid?

Healthy leadership doesn't promise safety, it promises stewardship. You are called to hold the moment, not master the outcome.

Every minute you spend spiraling in your head is a minute you're not stewarding the moment. Sometimes we call it "doing the work," when in reality, we're just delaying the decision.

The longer we wait, the heavier the decision becomes. Not because the facts changed, but because fear grew louder.

When the Past Hijacks the Present

One of the most unspoken causes of decision paralysis is trauma or memories, and not necessarily trauma in the traditional sense but unhealed past experiences that now masquerade as "gut feelings."

These moments don't just fade, they embed themselves. And left unexamined, they hijack the present.

Maybe you made a bold decision years ago and it failed and now you avoid risk at all costs. Maybe you were punished for speaking up in a previous job, so now you stay silent in meetings. Maybe a mentor betrayed your trust, so you second-guess yourself in every decision.

Instead of learning to grow in discernment, the moment planted a belief that you can't trust anyone…not even yourself.

And the result? You become a leader who lives in fear, decides in fear, and leads from fear instead of from a whole place.

🖉 Leadership Reflection: Your Decision-Making Profile

Take a few moments and consider:

- Where do you tend to get stuck when making decisions? Fear of failure, fear of judgment, perfectionism?
- What decisions are you currently avoiding? What would happen if you moved forward anyway?
- What past moment in leadership made you question your instincts? How might that still be affecting you?
- Are you more likely to pivot too soon or persevere too long?

Wholeness doesn't mean you never hesitate. It means you've learned how to move anyway.

The cost of indecision is rarely just missed opportunity. It's delayed growth. It's eroded confidence. It's the slow quieting of a leader's voice until they're unsure if they can trust it at all.

But you can.

Your voice, your wisdom, your spirit, it's needed. And while you may not always feel 100% sure, you can be sure of this:

You were never called to lead from fear. You were called to lead from fullness.

And the next time paralysis shows up? Don't wrestle it to the ground. Just take one step forward.

That's how bold decisions begin…with the decision to move.

Chapter 4 Takeaways: Overcoming Decision Paralysis

- Paralysis is not about indecision, it's about fear. And fear must be named before it can be neutralized.
- You don't need perfect certainty to move forward. You need clarity, courage, and a willingness to learn along the way.
- Sometimes perseverance is faithful. Sometimes pivoting is. Wisdom helps you tell the difference.
- Overthinking is a form of self-protection. But leadership requires action, even when you feel unsure.
- Your past can inform your decisions, but it doesn't have to control them. Healing makes room for better instincts.

"

Conviction isn't about being loud, it's about being anchored. Leaders who know who they are don't chase applause. They carry clarity."

CHAPTER 5

Leading with Conviction

It's one thing to make a decision. It's another thing to stand in it. There's a quiet kind of war that happens in leadership. It's the war between doing what's right and doing what's easy. The tension between choosing conviction over comfort, clarity over consensus, and truth over people-pleasing. And for many leaders, this battle doesn't happen in public, it happens in their minds, in their hearts, in the quiet before the announcement, the meeting, the confrontation.

Conviction is not stubbornness. It's not ego. It's not being unwilling to change. Conviction is clarity that has been tested and still stands. It's the internal assurance that says, Even if no one claps, even if they push back, I know this is the right direction.

Conviction doesn't make leadership easier. It makes it real.

The Power of Confidence in Decision-Making

Confidence is often misunderstood. We assume it's volume, posture, charisma. But true leadership confidence is not a look, it's an anchor. It's the steady presence that shows up when storms rise. It doesn't have to shout. It just doesn't move. Confident leaders aren't immune to doubt, they've just learned how to quiet the voices that don't belong in the decision-making room.

Confidence in decision-making isn't about being 100% sure. It's about being rooted in your process. You did the work. You weighed the facts. You checked in with your values. You listened. You prayed. You've come to peace even if it's still hard. When you make decisions from that place, your leadership tone changes. You're no longer defensive. You're no longer swayed by every new opinion. You can listen without being led off course. You can adjust without losing yourself.

This kind of confidence is what keeps a team anchored. When the leader is anxious, the culture is anxious. But when the leader is calm, even in chaos, it creates stability.

There's a confidence that comes from experience. But there's also a confidence that comes from alignment. When your decision aligns with your identity, your values, your vision, and your spirit you don't need approval to move forward. You just move.

How to Stand Firm in Tough Choices

Not all decisions will be met with applause. In fact, some of the most important decisions you'll ever make will be misunderstood at first. Whole leaders know this, and make them anyway.

Standing firm doesn't mean being inflexible. It means being faithful to the assignment you carry, and knowing how to communicate it with clarity, empathy, and ease. Think of Moses. He wasn't the most eloquent speaker. He didn't want the role. But when God told him to lead, he obeyed. And obedience often meant leading people who didn't want to be led, making decisions that were unpopular, standing between what was and what could be. Sound familiar?

Leadership will ask you to make decisions that cost you:

- Relationships with people who preferred you when you were agreeable.
- Comfort that came from staying silent.

- Temporary peace that comes from avoiding tension.

But here's the truth: avoiding hard decisions never creates peace. It just delays the conflict and multiplies the cost.

I once coached a principal who had to remove a long-tenured team member. Everyone loved this person. But her performance was hurting students and creating dysfunction. The leader wrestled with the choice for weeks. When he finally made it, the backlash came immediately… emails, rumors, passive resistance.

But six months later? Morale improved. Student success increased. And the culture finally began to heal. The leader told me, "I hated the process, but I've never been more sure of who I am." That is the moment as leaders we all look forward to. The moment it all makes sense.

That's conviction. It's painful, but it's clarifying. And here's the truth: if you don't stand firm, the loudest voice in the room will lead your organization. And it won't be yours.

Communicating Decisions with Clarity and Strength

Making the decision is only half the battle. Communicating it is what builds or breaks trust.

People don't just want to know what you've decided, they want to understand why.

Not in exhaustive detail, but in a way that connects the dots between vision and action. Your team deserves to know the story behind the strategy. Whole leaders understand this well. When your team seeks clarity, they aren't questioning your authority or your ability to lead.

They're trying to lean into the vision without sinking the ship. Helping them understand why empowers them to row in the same direction with purpose, not just compliance.

Clarity creates safety. Even if people don't agree with your decision, they can respect your process if they trust your integrity.

Here's what that sounds like:

- "After prayer, reflection, and feedback, I've come to this decision."
- "This move aligns with our core values, even though it's tough."
- "I know this may be difficult to receive. Here's how I got here, and here's what comes next."

What makes a decision hard to follow is not the decision itself, it's the ambiguity around it. Whole leaders communicate with humility and conviction. They don't over-explain. They don't manipulate. They don't throw others under the bus. They simply tell the truth with strength and grace.

The strength is in the clarity. The grace is in the tone.

Leading from Identity, Not Insecurity

At some point, every leader must confront the quiet question: Why do I need them to agree with me so badly?

If we're honest, much of our indecision, our over-apologizing, our watering down of truth comes from insecurity. We fear losing love, approval, or position. So we shrink, soften, or delay what we know we need to say.

But leaders who are rooted in identity don't need external affirmation to validate their internal knowing. They unapologetically know who they are, not from a place of pride, but from a place of wholeness. Your identity is not your role. It's not your performance. It's not your approval rating. Your identity is who you are when no one is clapping and you still show up.

Leading from insecurity creates culture rot. People can sense when your decisions are performative or passive-aggressive. Insecure leadership creates emotional confusion. One day you're confident, the next you're backpedaling. It's hard to follow someone whose identity is shifting with every reaction they receive.

But when you lead from identity?

- You don't chase applause.
- You don't panic when challenged.
- You don't second-guess your convictions just because they're not popular.

Instead, you move with quiet assurance. And that steadiness becomes contagious.

There will come a moment, if it hasn't already, when you must choose: comfort or conviction. And in that moment, your leadership will be defined not by how easy the choice is, but by how rooted you are when the choice costs something.

Conviction will not always make you popular. But it will make you clear. It will make you trustworthy. And over time, it will make you unshakable.

You don't have to lead loudly. You just have to lead, anchored.

🖋 Leadership Check-In: Conviction in Practice

Take a moment to reflect:

- What decision do I need to make, but haven't, because I'm afraid of the reaction?
- Am I leading this team, or are they leading me through pressure?
- Do I communicate my decisions clearly, or leave room for confusion?
- When I feel resistance, do I shrink, get louder, or stay steady?
- Is my leadership rooted in identity, or shaped by insecurity?

These are not easy questions. But asking them will make you a more honest and whole leader.

Chapter 5 Takeaways: Leading with Conviction

- Conviction is not about being stubborn, it's about being anchored in clarity and calling.
- Confidence in decision-making comes from alignment, not arrogance.
- Some of your most important decisions will be misunderstood. Make them anyway.
- How you communicate your decision matters as much as the decision itself.
- Whole leaders don't lead from insecurity. They lead from identity, and that steadiness builds trust.

"

If you're not taking time to refill, what you pour will cost more than what it's worth."

CHAPTER 6

What's In Your Cup

Leadership is not just about what you do, it's about what you carry. Every leader walks into the room with a full cup. That cup holds your thoughts, your tendencies, your past experiences, your stress, your strengths, your unhealed wounds, and your values. You can smile. You can perform. You can recite the mission with clarity. But when pressure comes—when something bumps you—whatever is in the cup spills.

This is one of the most powerful exercises I do with leaders, from executives to educators, from teens to seasoned pastors. I ask them to imagine holding a full cup of water. I gently bump their arm. Water spills out. Then I ask: Why did the water spill? They answer: Because you bumped me. But the truth is...the water spilled because there was water in the cup.

The bump just revealed it.

Every leader gets bumped. The email that wasn't professional. The team member who missed the deadline. The board member who questioned your strategy. The student who disrespected you in front of the room. The child who won't stop pushing your buttons. The bump is inevitable. But what flows out when you're bumped? Defensiveness? Sharpness? Control? Silence? Passive aggression? Perfectionism? Rage? Or... clarity. Patience. Wisdom. Vision. Discernment.

The bump doesn't create your response. It exposes it.

And in leadership, people aren't just watching your polished presentations, they're watching what spills out of you when pressure hits.

One of my favorite passages is a Proverb which states: *"Out of the heart flows the issues of life."* That's not just a verse. That's a leadership blueprint. In corporate spaces, we love data dashboards and KPIs. We measure output and behavior. But how often do we measure what's inside the cup?

If your inner world is filled with anxiety, fear, and control, you'll lead with urgency, micromanagement, and burnout. If it's filled with insecurity, comparison, and scarcity, you'll overcompensate, overcorrect, and under-trust. If it's filled with unhealed wounds, you'll interpret feedback as rejection and lead from a protective shell. But if your cup is filled with wholeness, values, wisdom, and grace, you'll lead with peace, even when the heat is on.

What's in your cup is what your people experience.

Not just your words, but your reactions.

Not just your decisions, but your tone.

Not just your strategy, but your spirit.

Let's get practical. You're in a team meeting. The numbers are off. Deadlines are missed. Everyone's on edge. The leader walks in. She's clearly irritated. She slams her notebook, sighs, and begins questioning people sharply. The team tightens up. Ideas shrink. Innovation freezes. No one felt safe, because what spilled out of her wasn't just about the numbers…it was about what was already in the cup: pressure, frustration, maybe fear or a need to control.

Same scenario. Different leader. He walks in. Addresses the issue with urgency—but calm. He invites solutions. He names the tension, but not in a way that blames. His presence sets the tone: *We're under pressure, but we're still aligned. Let's figure it out together.* What spilled out of him? Confidence. Groundedness. Ownership. Same bump. Different contents.

Leadership doesn't clock out at 5 p.m. What's in your cup at work is likely what's in your cup at home. You snap at your partner because you had a long day. You bark at your kids over a small mess. You withdraw from friends because you're overwhelmed. The bump wasn't the problem. It's what was already inside that needed attention. You can't keep blaming the bump. At some point, you have to ask: *What have I been carrying that keeps spilling over onto the people I am called to love and lead?*

This chapter is not about shame. It's about awareness. It's about ownership. Because here's the truth: You can only pour what's already in you. And if you're not taking time to refill, to reflect, to release, to be restored… then eventually, what you pour will cost more than what it's worth. You can have the most powerful vision, the sharpest pitch deck, the most articulate strategy… but if what's inside you is toxic, overwhelmed, or unhealed, eventually it will show.

Leadership leaks.

So what can you do? Start your day with reflection…not reaction.

- Before emails, check your emotions. Ask: *What am I carrying today? What's heavy? What's unresolved?*
- End your day with awareness. Ask: *Did I lead from alignment today or anxiety? Did I create safety or react from stress?*

- Schedule "cup checks." Set regular time to assess your emotional, spiritual, and physical state.
- Don't wait until burnout hits. Own your spills. When you respond poorly, acknowledge it. Go back and clean it up. That's leadership too.

The Leadership Audit: What's In Your Cup?

- What's currently filling your internal cup?
- When you're triggered, what tends to spill out?
- What environments tend to bump you most?
- How do you respond when someone else spills?
- What rhythms help you refill your cup in a healthy way?

Chapter 6 Takeaways: What's In Your Cup

- What spills out of you under pressure was already in you.
- You don't get to control the bump, but you do control what fills your cup.
- Self-awareness is not soft, it's strategic.
- Emotionally whole leaders don't lead perfectly, they lead honestly.
- When your cup is filled with peace, wisdom, and healing, your leadership becomes an overflow, not a performance.

“

Your mistake doesn't disqualify you. It reveals what you're now equipped to lead others through.

CHAPTER 7

Learning from Mistakes

There's a moment every leader will face when the plan didn't work, the conversation went sideways, or the outcome didn't meet expectations. And at that moment, the silence is loud. The second-guessing gets heavy. You might question whether you're cut out for this, whether you're losing credibility, or whether anyone even sees the weight you carry behind closed doors.

Welcome to the classroom of mistakes, not the classroom we ask for, but the one that builds us into leaders worth following.

Most leadership books celebrate the wins. They highlight big decisions that paid off. But what often goes unsaid is how many decisions, especially the brave ones, are born through error. Through recovery. Through sitting in the tension of what didn't go right.

We need more leaders who are fluent in failure. Not because we aspire to fail, but because we refuse to be defined by it.

The Misconception of Failure

Somewhere along the way, leaders were taught that making a mistake meant weakness. That public error reduced authority. That vulnerability made you less respected. But the truth is, how a leader handles their mistakes is often the most defining proof of their integrity.

Mistakes don't destroy trust…concealing them does.

According to the Edelman Trust Barometer, employees who strongly agree that their organization is transparent are 8.9 times more likely to trust their leadership.

When we hide our errors, we create a culture of perfectionism and fear. Our teams mirror that same posture, avoiding risk, staying silent, and protecting reputation over impact. That's not leadership. That's performance. But when a leader models recovery, the culture changes. They communicate something powerful: you don't have to be perfect to be excellent,you just have to be honest.

Behind every misstep is something trying to get your attention. Maybe it's a pattern you didn't notice before. Maybe it's a wound that still needs healing. Maybe it's a belief system, about yourself, others, or leadership, that needs to be rewritten.

That's where the Leadership Pathway comes back into play.

While leadership is often measured through behavior, culture, and results, this book argues that deeper drivers are at work: belief systems, emotional healing, identity, and personal experiences. Ignoring these inner dimensions leads to shallow leadership. Engaging them builds emotionally whole, transformational leaders.

So when you make a mistake, don't just ask "What happened?" Ask:

- What did this outcome reveal about my beliefs?
- Was I leading from fear, insecurity, or the need for approval?
- Was I reactive, rushed, or trying to protect an outdated version of myself?

Because mistakes aren't just about the situation...they're about what the situation exposes in us.

A Story of Redemptive Leadership

I once coached a leader who prided himself on efficiency. Quick decisions, fast delegation, minimal emotion. But during a restructure, he cut a department without consulting the team leads. He believed the data justified the decision.

What he didn't realize was that this team was already navigating burnout and change fatigue. They didn't need another top-down directive. They needed a conversation.

Within weeks, morale plummeted. Team members disengaged. Some left altogether.

"I didn't see it coming," he told me. "I thought I was doing the right thing."

And in many ways, he was at least from a strategy standpoint. But his mistake wasn't rooted in malice. It was rooted in a disconnect between efficiency and empathy. Between strategy and story. Between data and people.

The real redemption wasn't in fixing the restructure. It was in how he owned the impact. He met with each team member individually, listened to their pain, acknowledged his oversight, and invited their voice into future decisions. That team didn't just recover, they began to trust again. Not because of the correction, but because of the courage it took to own the miss.

Mistakes can break trust…or rebuild it in ways that success never could.

Recovering Without Retreating

One of the most dangerous responses to a leadership mistake is retreat. Not the kind where you physically leave, but where you emotionally disengage. You stop contributing, stop trusting yourself, stop taking healthy risks. You start doubting everything and become overly cautious. You become quieter not because you've grown wiser, but because you've grown afraid.

But leadership requires presence, even after pain. Especially after pain.

When you retreat, you give the mistake more power than it deserves. You let shame become the narrator. But when you recover—really recover—you take ownership of the mistake without letting it own you.

You don't need to shrink to be self-aware. You don't have to disappear to prove you're remorseful. You don't have to lead smaller to lead better.

You recover by showing up again this time, with more wisdom, more clarity, and more grace.

Mistakes as Mirrors, Not Labels

You must remember: mistakes are mirrors, not labels. They reflect what needs attention, not what defines you. But many leaders internalize failure as identity.

Thoughts like:

- "I'm not good at this."
- "They don't trust me anymore."
- "Maybe I'm not cut out for leadership."

These lies burrow deep and quietly shape how we lead. But wholeness says: "This mistake is information not identity."

So when a decision goes wrong, pause and reflect:

- What did this expose about my leadership pattern?
- Was I people-pleasing, overcorrecting, rushing, avoiding?
- What do I need to heal or release so I don't repeat it?

This is about self-leadership. Emotionally whole leaders don't avoid hard truths, they integrate them. They let mistakes sharpen their discernment, strengthen their systems, and deepen their humility.

A Deeper Way to Teach Others

When you've walked through leadership failure and healed, you become one of the most powerful leaders in the room. Not because you're flawless, but because you're trustworthy.

You've missed the mark and course-corrected. You've stood back up with integrity. And because you've done the work, you can now walk others through their own missteps without ego, judgment, or shame.

People don't need perfect leaders. They need present ones.

Leaders who have felt the sting, owned the moment, healed it, and now use that wisdom to move forward.

🖋 Leadership Pathway in Motion

Let's bring it back to the Leadership Pathway framework.

Many leaders respond to failure by changing behavior, people-pleasing more, controlling more, striving more. But behavior alone won't get to the root. The real work is deeper.

Ask yourself:

- What belief made me think I had to get this perfect?
- What past moment taught me that mistakes equal rejection?
- What inner vow made me afraid to ask for help?

This is the work beneath the work. When we avoid it, we end up chasing applause instead of walking in wholeness. And what results? Leadership marked by control, silence, performance.

But when we lean in and address the real drivers—beliefs, wounds, identity—then we step into what this book is really about: emotionally whole leadership, rooted in wisdom, humility, and clarity.

Leadership Audit: Learning From Mistakes

Take a moment. Reflect honestly.

- What is one mistake I've made in leadership that still echoes in my mind?
- What did I learn from it? About the situation and about myself?
- Did I shrink, shift, or sabotage after that moment?
- What part of me needs compassion, not criticism, to fully recover?
- How has this shaped my pace, my people, or my values?

Chapter 7 Takeaways

Let's not close with bullets..but with breath.

I want you to know this…

Mistakes don't make you less. They make you more aware.

You don't lose credibility by being human. You build it by being honest.

The goal isn't flawless leadership. It's faithful, fearless, and whole leadership.

So learn. Reflect. Integrate. Then stand back up stronger than before.

Because Leaders Make Decisions, and the best ones learn from every single one.

PART III

Wholeness That Multiplies

An Author's Note

The next few chapters shift in tone. You may notice shorter lines. A slower pace. A coaching rhythm. That's intentional.

This is where the book moves from building clarity in you… to helping you carry that clarity forward.

From insight to embodiment.

From internal healing to external legacy.

These pages were written not just to teach, but to anchor.

To slow you down.

To remind you of who you are.

You've done the work.

Now, let's walk it forward…together.

“

Broken systems are often the result of broken people in charge of them”

CHAPTER 8

Leading Forward from Wholeness

Wholeness is not the end of your journey as a leader…it's the beginning of a new one.

Once you've looked inward, healed wounds, faced fears, and released perfectionism, your leadership takes on a new shape.

Not louder.

Not faster.

Not shinier.

But truer.

More grounded.

More transformative.

Firmly planted.

You no longer lead from pressure. You lead from presence.

This chapter is about what happens when leaders stop chasing and start embodying. When you stop trying to outrun your past and start leading from your healed identity. When the need to prove is replaced by a steady knowing of who you are, what you carry, and where you're going.

Can I tell you? The greatest shift in my leadership wasn't a new strategy. It was becoming whole enough to lead without needing to prove myself.

This is leading forward from wholeness. It's the moment when you look up, and it all makes sense.

Redefining Success Through the Lens of Inner Transformation

In corporate spaces, success is often defined by outcomes: growth, profitability, visibility, and influence. In ministry, it's often defined by reach, response, or spiritual fruit. In educational spaces, it may be numbers, academic benchmarks, or behavioral compliance. Across every industry, we're taught to chase output often at the expense of inner clarity.

But when a leader becomes whole, the metrics start to shift.

You begin to realize that success isn't just about what you build, it's about what builds you.

It's not just about what you produce, it's about who you become in the process.

You're no longer driven by the applause or burdened by the outcome.

You begin asking better questions:

- Am I leading in alignment with my values?
- Are the people around me flourishing…or just functioning?
- Am I modeling the kind of life I want my team to believe is possible?

Inner transformation reframes everything.

You build differently. You move slower…but more intentionally. You speak softer…but with greater weight.

You begin to notice that what used to feel like leadership was actually performance. And what feels like peace now looks like wisdom.

That's the pivot. That's what happens when you begin to lead from a healed place.

You stop measuring your worth by what gets done. You begin to lead from a deeper center—anchored, honest, and free.

How Whole Leaders Transform Culture

If you've ever walked into a room and felt the presence of a grounded leader, you know what I'm talking about.

It's not just charisma.

It's clarity.

It's not control.

It's capacity.

It's not dominance.

It's discernment.

Whole leaders carry something that can't be imitated: a non-anxious presence that shifts the emotional atmosphere.

Wholeness has ripple effects. It doesn't just affect you, it affects the room. The decisions. The tone. The culture.

When a leader is whole:

- Psychological safety increases.
- Authentic conversations emerge.
- Creative risk-taking becomes more common.
- Trust becomes the default setting.

People don't have to guess your motives or anticipate your reactions. They know where you stand because you do.

This is the leadership the next generation is longing for.

Especially in spaces where burnout, performance fatigue, and disillusionment have become normalized.

We don't need louder leaders, we need clearer ones. Leaders who know who they are and don't need chaos to feel important. Leaders who restore what previous models eroded: trust, humanity, and health.

Whole leaders rebuild trust. And trust rebuilds culture.

Rebuilding Systems, Not Just Solving Problems

Broken systems are often the result of broken people in charge of them.

When leaders lead from fear, the systems they design become reactive. When they lead from insecurity, the culture becomes toxic. When they lead from ego, the structure rewards performance over wellness.

That's why surface-level problem solving rarely works. It treats the fruit without addressing the root.

But whole leaders don't just manage problems they reimagine possibilities.

They start asking courageous questions:

- Why do we reward burnout and call it excellence?
- Why is our decision-making reactive instead of reflective?

- Are we building structures that serve people, or using people to protect structures?

I once worked with an executive team who couldn't understand why retention was plummeting despite good pay and impressive benefits.

But what they couldn't see, until we unpacked it, was that the system had been built around one person's emotional wounds.

Her fear of failure had created a culture of micromanagement. Her unresolved perfectionism had translated into unsustainable expectations.

The culture wasn't broken because of policy. It was broken because of pain.

Once she began to lead from a healing place, the system shifted. Not overnight but organically.

This is the invisible power of wholeness. It doesn't scream…but it shapes everything.

Integrating Healing Into Your Leadership Vision

Healing isn't a soft skill. It's a leadership strategy.

It's not a detour, it's the foundation.

Because anything you build apart from wholeness will eventually ask you to trade your peace for performance.

And no mission, no matter how big, is worth your soul.

So what does it mean to integrate healing into your leadership vision?

It means:

- Making room for reflection, not just reaction.
- Building cultures where vulnerability is honored, not hidden.
- Modeling rest, not as a privilege, but as a principle.
- Letting mistakes become data, not disqualifiers.
- Returning often to one guiding question:

Am I leading from healing or from habit?

Your leadership vision becomes more than a PowerPoint or a mission statement. It becomes a lived embodiment of what's possible when leaders prioritize presence over performance.

You begin to embody the very thing you hope to produce in others: Clarity. Alignment. Resilience. Joy.

That's the power of wholeness, it doesn't just teach. It transforms.

🖊 Leadership Audit: Am I Leading from Wholeness?

Take a moment. Slow down. Be honest, not critical. Reflect on these:

- Am I leading from alignment, or from adrenaline?
- Do I feel grounded in who I am, or constantly proving that I belong?
- Is my culture emotionally safe, or emotionally silent?
- Do I lead with rest in mind, or only results?
- When was the last time I paused to check in with me?

This audit isn't about performance. It's about presence. It's not about scoring, it's about noticing. Because what you notice, you can change. And what you change, you can heal.

Chapter 8 Takeaways

- Wholeness is not the absence of pressure, it's the presence of peace under it.
- Whole leaders aren't just better decision-makers, they're better people-makers.
- They create culture through consistency.
- They build legacy through values.
- They lead forward, not from fear, but from fullness.

You don't lead from what's missing anymore. You lead forward from what's been healed.

"

Healing doesn't make you less of a leader, it makes you the kind of leader others can trust, follow, and flourish under."

CHAPTER 9

The Benefits of Healing in Leadership

Most leadership books don't talk about healing. They talk about scaling. About vision. About goals, strategy, and execution. They teach you how to perform under pressure, communicate in crisis, and delegate tasks. And while all of that has its place, none of it means much if the person leading is silently unraveling on the inside.

Healing may not be the headline of most leadership curriculums, but it is the quiet key behind long-term influence.

Because unhealed leaders will always leak pain, no matter how polished their presence.

They will micromanage out of fear, control out of insecurity, or retreat in shame. Not because they're bad people, but because they're people carrying wounds they never paused long enough to name.

But when leaders do the work? When they tend to their inner world with intentionality, compassion, and courage?

Something extraordinary begins to happen.

The reality is...healing clears the fog.

What used to feel confusing becomes clear, not because the decisions get easier, but because *you* get more honest. You stop second-guessing yourself every time someone disagrees. You stop making decisions to please people. You know your values. You trust your voice. You operate from alignment instead of anxiety.

Clarity is a natural byproduct of emotional wholeness.

So is compassion. You begin to lead others the way you've learned to lead yourself with patience, grace, and truth. You no longer need perfection from your team. You look for progress. You make space for humanity. You correct with care and challenge without condemnation. Compassion becomes a leadership superpower, not a liability.

And then...creativity flows. When your brain is not tied up in self-doubt or emotional exhaustion, it has room to imagine. To innovate. To birth new ideas. Whole leaders don't just regurgitate trends. They create paths no one else has seen, because their minds are clear and their hearts are steady.

Reducing Burnout and Enhancing Resilience

You know what burns leaders out?

Trying to fix everything while ignoring yourself.

Leading with chronic responsibility but no restoration. Showing up for everyone while secretly disappearing inside. Carrying unresolved grief and calling it grit. That's what leads to burnout, not the work itself, but the way we carry it when we're disconnected from ourselves.

According to Gallup, 76% of employees experience burnout at least sometimes, and 28% report being burned out 'very often' or 'always.

Healing doesn't remove pressure...but it changes your posture under it.

You no longer feel the need to say yes to everything. You stop using work as a distraction. You get honest about your limits and no longer see rest as weakness. You set boundaries and honor them without guilt.

That's not laziness. That's legacy-building.

Resilience is not just your capacity to endure, it's your capacity to recover. And when you've done the work of healing, recovery becomes part of your rhythm, not just your reaction to burnout.

Building Authentic Trust and Emotional Safety in Teams

So, how do we rebuild trust and emotional safety in teams? First, we have to understand that people don't just trust competent leaders, they trust *consistent* ones.

They trust the ones who show up the same way in public and private. The ones who listen without needing to dominate. The ones who don't change personalities depending on the pressure in the room.

Healing produces emotional safety. And emotional safety is the birthplace of high-performing teams.

When a team knows they won't be shamed for failure, innovation increases. When people are allowed to feel, creativity blossoms. When leadership is rooted in humanity, loyalty grows not out of fear, but from mutual respect.

And let's be clear: emotional safety is not softness. It's strength. It's what allows people to speak truth, take ownership, and lean into the hard conversations that actually move things forward.

Whole leaders don't make emotional safety optional. They make it cultural.

Creating Sustainable Results Through Emotionally Mature Leadership

Anyone can create short-term wins through charisma or control. But long-term fruit? That takes maturity.

It takes a leader who knows how to manage emotions in a crisis and hold vision when the outcome isn't clear. A leader who doesn't implode when challenged, or disappear when things don't go their way. A leader who can absorb feedback without defensiveness and adjust without shame.

That's emotional maturity.

And emotionally mature leaders produce sustainable results because they don't have to rebuild after emotional explosions or ego-driven fallout.

They can course-correct in real time. They can shift a team without breaking its spirit. They can hold authority without becoming authoritarian. That kind of leadership is rare, but it's what the future requires.

The world doesn't need more reactive leaders.
It needs more healed ones.

🖋 Leadership Audit: How Is Healing Showing Up in My Leadership?

Ask yourself, not to critique, but to locate:

- Do I feel clear or cloudy when making decisions?
- Am I responding to pressure with presence, or panic?
- Do people feel safe to fail under my leadership?

- Am I leading with emotional maturity, or emotional urgency?
- What personal healing would allow me to lead with more grace and less control?

You won't get it perfect. That's not the goal.
But awareness is the first step to leadership that doesn't just work, it **lasts**.

Chapter 9 Takeaways

Healing is not a detour on your leadership journey…it's the engine behind your longevity.

It's how you gain clarity without needing control.
How you build trust without manipulation.
How you create without burning out.
How you lead with fire, without constantly catching fire.

A whole leader can weather storms without sinking.
Can build results without losing their soul.
Can challenge others without crushing them.
Can be soft enough to feel and strong enough to stand.

Because at the core of sustainable leadership is this truth:
Your healing is not just about you. It's about everyone who experiences the fruit of your leadership.

CHAPTER 10

Becoming a Model of Possibility

What happens when a leader decides to be the evidence of what's possible?

Not the exception.

Not the anomaly.

Not the superhuman.

But the embodiment of what happens when healing and leadership collide.

This chapter isn't about a new strategy. It's a reminder: you are becoming the very thing someone else is praying exists.

When you choose healing, when you lead from wholeness, when you make emotionally sound decisions you stop merely managing roles and start modeling transformation. And people notice. They notice not because you shout louder, but because your presence speaks before your mouth ever opens.

You become a walking permission slip for others to lead differently.

It's one thing to talk about leadership theory. It's another to live the story of what healed leadership looks like in real time.

This doesn't mean you have all the answers. It means you've stopped pretending you do. It means you lead with integrity, not performance. With values, not vibes. With peace, not pretense.

Transformation is magnetic. People are drawn to leaders who are human and honest, who own their scars and speak from wholeness, not from a need to prove.

You become the "before and after" picture no one knew they needed: The one who used to overthink everything... but now leads from clarity. The one who carried fear of failure... but now moves with grounded courage. The one who used to confuse hustle with worth... but now leads from rest.

You don't have to preach it. Your presence says enough.

Mentoring Others Through Your Growth

Whole leaders don't hoard wisdom, they multiply it.

When you've been through something and come out the other side—not perfect, but transformed—you carry a kind of weight that makes others lean in. People trust what you've lived more than what you've read.

That's why healed leaders become the best mentors. Not because they have perfect resumes, but because they've been through the fire, and they're not ashamed to talk about it.

They don't teach from theory. They guide from experience.

Mentorship becomes more than passing down knowledge. It becomes impartation. It becomes sacred ground where you look someone in the eye and say: *"I've been there. And you're going to make it, too."*

This kind of leadership doesn't just change workplaces. It heals people. It raises up a generation of leaders who no longer think they have to choose between excellence and humanity, strength and softness, clarity and compassion.

Embracing the Future with Courage and Hope

One of the greatest gifts of healing is that it releases you from the grip of your past.

You stop making decisions based on pain, shame, or trauma. You stop defining your capacity by what hurt you. You stop leading as a reaction to what you've lost. Instead, you start leaning into what's ahead with courage and hope.

Courage says, "I may not have all the details, but I know who I am."

Hope says, "I've seen what's broken…but I still believe in what's possible."

And together, courage and hope become the fuel for your future.

You begin dreaming again, not from ego, but from alignment. You set vision from a place of identity, not insecurity. You don't need to prove yourself anymore, so you're free to build something that reflects the best of you, because it's coming from the healed parts of you.

This is the leadership the world needs.
Not perfect. Not pressure-filled. But possible.
Because once someone sees what's possible in you, they start to believe in what's possible for them.

Let's be clear, this journey is not about arrival.

Wholeness is not a destination you check off. It's not a moment you "finally reach." It's a foundation you continue to build on, return to, and protect.

It is the deep, anchored place you come back to when the pressure rises. The filter you run decisions through when fear tries to hijack the process. The truth you ground yourself in when noise tries to define you.

It's the foundation that holds your leadership steady when the spotlight is bright or the shadows feel long.

You'll still face hard days.
You'll still have to make decisions that stretch you.
You'll still be human.

But now…
You'll be human with tools.
You'll be whole with wisdom.
You'll be a leader with legacy, not just success.

That's what this whole journey has been about, not just learning to lead, but learning to live as someone who is whole, healed, and unafraid to make decisions from that place.

Leadership Audit: Am I a Living Model of What's Possible?

- Do others feel more free, more grounded, or more safe after working with me?
- Am I mentoring from wisdom or managing from fear?
- Does my leadership invite others to become more of themselves, or less?
- Am I building legacy from wholeness, or from a need to prove?
- What would it look like to be the model I wish I had?

You don't need to be perfect to be powerful.
You just need to be whole enough to be real.

Chapter 10 Takeaways

You are not just leading tasks. You are shaping lives.
You are not just making decisions. You are making models.
You are not just building success. You are building legacy.

Whole leaders don't just produce impact.
They produce belief, belief in what's possible when leaders get free.

And when one leader chooses healing?
That freedom becomes contagious.

CHAPTER 11

Leading Others Through the Same Work

Wholeness doesn't end with you. In fact, it was never meant to.

The true mark of a transformed leader isn't just how well they lead it's how well they cultivate transformation in others. And once you've done the internal work, the next question becomes: *How do I help others rise without carrying them? How do I lead people into the same freedom I've fought for?*

The short answer? **By modeling it, not managing it.** The long answer? Let's walk it out.

Start with Your Presence, Not Your Plan

You don't need a new meeting agenda to introduce emotionally whole leadership. You need presence. When your team or staff begins to feel the difference in how you show up, how you respond, how you listen, how you navigate tension, they'll notice. People always notice when a leader becomes lighter but more grounded. Quieter but more impactful. Kinder but more clear.

You lead others into wholeness by embodying the work, not announcing it.

Before you host a culture session or book club, ask yourself:

- Am I practicing the values I'm inviting others into?
- Am I reacting less and regulating more?
- Am I leading from security, not surveillance?

Your transformation creates an invitation, and people are more likely to trust a leader who reflects the work rather than recites it.

One of the biggest mistakes leaders make when they begin their own healing journey is rushing their teams into vulnerability before the culture is ready. It's not that your team doesn't want to grow emotionally, they just want to know it's safe.

According to Amy C Edmondson, psychological safety is the belief that one can speak up without risk of punishment or humiliation and is the number one factor in high-performing teams.

Psychological safety comes first. That means:

- Listening more than you speak.
- Celebrating process, not perfection.
- Acknowledging your own mistakes without dumping your pain.
- Modeling emotional clarity without demanding emotional performance.

Your team needs to feel secure enough to reflect. And that security starts with how you lead under pressure.

Normalize the Conversation Without Forcing the Change

You can begin weaving this language into your leadership culture without forcing anyone into a therapy session.

Try phrases like:

- "Let's name what's underneath that reaction."
- "Are we leading from alignment or just urgency?"
- "Let's pause and check: Is this decision fear-driven or values-driven?"

You're not asking people to become emotional experts. You're asking them to become *emotionally aware.*

If you lead in a corporate setting, this might look like redefining performance metrics to include collaboration or self-awareness. In a ministry context, it might look like having team check-ins that ask *"How's your heart?"* not just *"Where's your output?"*

Coach with Questions, Not Control

One of the most powerful tools you can use is curiosity. When someone on your team reacts harshly, misses a deadline, or resists feedback, your job isn't to control the outcome…it's to coach the root.

Try asking:

- "What came up for you in that moment?"
- "Was that response based on today—or something deeper?"
- "What story might you be telling yourself here?"

These kinds of questions open the door to reflection without shame. You're not diagnosing them, you're helping them lead themselves better. That's what whole leaders do.

Resist the Savior Syndrome

Even as you guide others, you must remember: you are not responsible for someone else's healing. You can hold space. You can model clarity.

You can offer tools. But healing is a personal decision. Wholeness is an inside job.

What you *are* responsible for is the culture you create. So instead of fixing people, build systems that make healing possible. Instead of controlling outcomes, normalize feedback, rest, growth, and grace.

The Legacy of Wholeness

The world doesn't need more brilliant leaders with broken hearts. It needs leaders like you, those who lead from peace, not panic. From identity, not insecurity. From vision, not ego.

If this book helped you see yourself more clearly, now it's time to help others do the same. Whether you're leading a boardroom or a Bible study, a faculty team or a startup, let your presence become the permission.

Let your leadership become the proof.

You don't have to be perfect. Just present.
Not flawless, just faithful.
Not fearless, but *fearless enough* to go first.

🖋 Leadership Audit:

- Who on your team needs safety, not correction?
- Where might you be reacting instead of reflecting?
- What part of your current leadership structure supports wholeness, and what part undermines it?
- Are your people flourishing, or just functioning?

Chapter 11 Takeaways:

- You lead others into wholeness by embodying the work, not announcing it.
- Culture shifts when presence changes, not just policies.
- You're not responsible for someone's healing, but you are responsible for the systems you create.
- Whole leaders build whole cultures and whole cultures change lives.

Conclusion: Whole Leaders Change Everything

You've made it to the end...but this isn't the end. It's a beginning. A beginning for the kind of leadership the world is quietly begging for. Leadership that doesn't fracture under pressure. That doesn't require burnout to earn respect. That doesn't confuse performance with identity.

This isn't leadership that just looks good on a stage. This is leadership that holds steady in the quiet. The kind that pauses to breathe before reacting. That sees people, not just productivity. That can speak truth without shame and execute vision without ego. It's bold enough to pause. Healed enough to see clearly. Whole enough to build what actually lasts.

Because at the heart of every culture shift, team breakthrough, or visionary strategy, there is a decision. And behind every decision, there is a leader. A human being. With a story. With belief systems. With values. With scars. With influence. And those internal dynamics—those unseen drivers—don't vanish the moment someone gives you a title. In fact, they show up louder. The meeting table reveals them. The budget cuts expose them. The conflict draws them to the surface.

That's why this book didn't start with productivity or planning or performance. It started with the soul. Because culture is shaped by behavior, and behavior is shaped by belief. If you don't go to the root, the fruit will always be inconsistent. If you don't address the heart, the habits will always revert. If you don't confront the past, you will carry it into every future decision, no matter how forward-facing your calendar looks.

Leadership isn't just what you do. It's what you carry. And if you're not paying attention to what's in you, it will eventually affect what's around you. That's not weakness. That's wisdom. Because the real work of leadership is not just learning how to *lead others*. It's learning how to lead yourself with clarity, with courage, with emotional maturity, and with wholeness.

This is a different kind of leadership. It's not performative, it's grounded. It's not reactive, it's wise. It doesn't chase outcomes at the expense of people, or at the expense of your own health. It doesn't lead from a need to prove. It leads from a place of identity. It is anchored in values. It is steady under pressure. It doesn't break when the spotlight gets bright or the boardroom gets silent.

It knows how to say, "I don't know yet," without shame. It knows how to pivot when plans fall apart, how to pause when clarity is missing, how to name the real issue behind the resistance in the room. It knows how to set direction with discernment, not desperation. This kind of leadership doesn't just get wins in Q3. It lasts. It stabilizes teams, rebuilds trust, creates sustainable people-centered results. It protects innovation while preserving the soul of the people tasked with carrying it.

And yes, this kind of leadership changes lives. But it also changes spreadsheets. It drives metrics. It sustains systems. Because emotionally whole leaders don't just make wise decisions. They make better ones. Smarter ones. More collaborative. More strategic. More sustainable. They align vision with values. People with purpose. Strategy with soul.

And if you forget everything else, remember this:

You are not too broken to lead.
Your healing is not a detour, it's your foundation.
Your decisions don't have to be reactionary. They can be redemptive.
You don't have to hustle to prove. You can lead from peace.
And you don't have to have all the answers to walk in authority.

This isn't about being soft. It's about being solid.

The world is full of noise. It is craving leaders who are quiet on the inside, leaders who are steady, discerning, clear, and whole.

Legacy isn't just what you leave behind. It's what you normalize while you're here. You've now been equipped with a new lens. You've seen the power of emotionally sound decisions. You've explored the roots behind reactionary leadership. You've uncovered the patterns. You've faced the inner work. You've been challenged to lead from healing, not hustle.

Now it's your turn.

It's your turn to lead in a way that heals culture, not just drives it.
To make decisions that come from clarity, not chaos.
To challenge the next generation to prioritize their soul, not just their salary.
To make wholeness your strategy, not your afterthought.

Because at the end of the day, **Leaders Make Decisions**
But whole leaders?
They make the ones that change everything.

Appendix: Fearless Leadership Integration Toolkit

Executive Summary: If You Only Do One Thing This Month…

This is your high-impact activation guide, if time is limited, start here.

- **Daily Calibration (3 mins)**
    - What's influencing my decisions today—clarity or fear?
    - Am I showing up grounded or reactive?
    - What energy am I carrying into the room?
- **Weekly Reset**
    - Where did I lead from healing this week?
    - What decision did I delay that deserves movement?
- **High-Leverage Team Sync**
    - Ask: "Where do we need clarity, not just compliance?"
- **System Audit Prompt**
    - Are our systems built to protect people—or performance optics?
- **Bold Challenge**
    - Make one emotionally honest leadership decision, this week.

30-Day Leadership Calibration Plan

Designed for high-capacity leaders who want to operationalize wholeness.

Week 1: Awareness

- Day 1: Write it Out: Where do I feel most reactive as a leader?
- Day 3: Observe: What emotions arise in tension?
- Day 5: Name emotions without judgment.
- Day 7: Reflect: How does my past shape my leadership style?

Week 2: Alignment

- Day 9: Identify your top 5 leadership values.
- Day 10: Audit 3 decisions. Did they align?
- Day 12: Practice one act of authentic vulnerability.
- Day 14: Request feedback on your emotional leadership presence.

Week 3: Authority

- Day 16: Identify where you feel the need to prove yourself.
- Day 18: Practice saying, "I don't know yet" in one meeting.
- Day 19: Differentiate ego vs. identity.
- Day 21: Sketch a "decision pressure map" of how you respond under stress.

Week 4: Activation

- Day 23: Host a well-being check-in with your team.
- Day 25: Ask: What helps you feel safe here?
- Day 27: Review: Are we optimizing for people or metrics?
- Day 30: Write your personal "Leadership From Wholeness" declaration.

Wholeness Indicators for Strategic Leaders

You're leading from wholeness when...

- You pause before reacting.
- You hold tension without spiraling.
- You lead from values, not vibes.
- Your emotional tone is predictable, even under pressure.

Warning signs you're slipping into wounded leadership...

- Micromanagement disguised as excellence.
- You avoid feedback or reinterpret it as failure.
- Your emotional state is tied to results.
- You make decisions to be liked, not to lead

Team Sync Questions for Culture Reset

- What was the most clarifying or confronting idea from this book?
- Which belief about leadership have I outgrown?
- What decision have I been avoiding out of fear?
- What part of our culture needs to heal, not just improve?
- What leadership behavior do we reward that might be misaligned?

Tip: Use one of these in your next leadership off-site or 1:1 coaching check-in.

Weekly Performance Rhythm

Monday: Reflect

- Ask: How do I want to show up this week?
- What's unresolved emotionally?

Tuesday: Align

- Anchor one key decision to a core value.
- Affirm a team member's emotional effort.

Wednesday: Audit

- Midweek check-in: Am I leading from anxiety or awareness?
- Adjust one action to reflect alignment.

Thursday: Lead

- Make a courageous decision today.
- Model emotional honesty in a difficult moment.

Friday: Integrate

- Journal: Where did I lead from wholeness?
- What lesson needs to be carried into next week?

Coach's Corner: Full Reflection Question List

Collected for use in coaching, journaling, or team dialogue.

- What hidden weights are you carrying that no one sees but you? How are they affecting your decisions?
- When uncertainty clouds your leadership, what do you return to first, performance or presence?
- What area of your life are you asking others to model that you haven't mastered yourself?
- What blind spots do you sense in your leadership? When are you most likely to lead from reaction instead of wisdom?
- What's one area of emotional healing you've avoided? How is it affecting your leadership?
- What decision have you been circling lately? What's underneath your hesitation?
- What fear-based moment in your past might still be shaping how you make decisions today?
- What are you holding onto that might have served its purpose but no longer fits where you're going?
- What leadership memory might be masquerading as a "gut feeling" and blocking your progress?
- What was the last decision you made that cost you something? Would you still make it again?
- What's one decision you've delayed because you feared the fallout?
- What's in your cup right now? What emotional contents have been spilling when you're under pressure?

- What is your first instinct when you make a mistake? To explain it away, hide it, or learn from it? Why?
- What narrative have you attached to your last leadership misstep? Is it rooted in truth, or fear?

Micro Practices: Mini Moves That Shift Culture

Collected from every chapter to integrate with coaching and leadership routines.

- Reflect on a recent decision. Write down who it impacted, both directly and indirectly. What did your process teach others?
- What is one belief or behavior you know you need to confront in yourself to create safety for others?
- Think of a time recently when you were under pressure. What was your instinctive response? What would a regulated version of you have done differently?
- Write down a recent decision you delayed. Then answer honestly, what were you most afraid of in that moment?
- What is one area where you've been overestimating risk and underestimating reward?
- Write one decision you've been overthinking. Commit to one action you'll take this week to break the spiral.
- Think of a recent decision that required confidence. Write down what anchored you.
- Write out three values that define your identity, not your role.
- Recall the last time you were "bumped" as a leader. Write down exactly what spilled out. Then ask: Was that a true reflection of who I want to be?
- Reflect on a time when you missed the mark. Write out the story from your perspective and then from your team's. What shifts when you change the lens?
- Each morning this week, name what's fueling your leadership that day: fear, pressure, peace, purpose, or something else.

- At the end of the day, ask: "Did I lead from healing or habit?"
- Rewrite your leadership mission statement from a healed place.
- Schedule one hour weekly of "quiet clarity". No input, just you, a notebook, and reflection time.
- In your next meeting, ask the team to describe the emotional climate of the room using one word. Debrief gently and without defensiveness.

A Final Word…

To The Leader Reading This,

Thank you. Not just for turning the pages, but for turning toward yourself.

You could have picked up a quick guide, a checklist, or another book on how to lead with tactics. But instead, you chose to do the deeper work. The inner work. The work that doesn't always get seen, but always gets felt.

My hope isn't that you agree with every word. My hope is that you saw yourself somewhere in these pages, and gave yourself permission to grow, to heal, and to lead again from a whole place.

This book isn't the finish line. It's a mirror. A map. A moment to say: you don't have to lead from fear, performance, burnout, or borrowed blueprints. You were never meant to.

You were meant to lead from fullness. From peace. From presence. From the kind of inner truth that doesn't shout to be heard, because it already knows who it is.

So let this not be the end, but the beginning of a bolder chapter in your leadership. Keep showing up. Keep recalibrating. Keep making decisions that honor the kind of leader you're becoming.

I believe in your leadership. I believe in your legacy. And I'm grateful you let me walk part of the journey with you.

Let's keep going,
Dr. Tiana

About The Author

Dr. Tiana P. Clemons is a multi-dimensional leader, speaker, and coach with a dynamic blend of academic excellence and real-world experience. She holds a B.S. in Health Sciences, an M.Div. in Christian Ministry, and a D.Min. in Pastoral Counseling, along with certifications in leadership, empathy, active listening, and motivational communication from her successful corporate career.With a track record of coaching 500+ professionals in career advancement and leading high-impact university campaigns, Dr. Tiana now dedicates her work to helping purpose-driven leaders create high-performing teams, lead with emotional intelligence, and thrive personally and professionally. Known for her vibrant presence and deep emotional insight, she inspires people to move beyond comfort zones, confront limiting beliefs, and lead with confidence, clarity, and purpose. Her mission is simple: to help leaders lead from wholeness and build cultures where growth isn't just possible, it's inevitable.

"

Lead from wholeness. Decide from courage. Impact from overflow.

Citations

*Bradberry, T., & Greaves, J. (2009). *Emotional Intelligence 2.0*. TalentSmart.*

*Brown, B. (2015). *Rising Strong*. Spiegel & Grau.*

*Edmondson, A. C. (2018). *The Fearless Organization: Creating Psychological Safety in the Workplace for Learning, Innovation, and Growth*. Wiley.*

*Edelman Trust Barometer. (2022). *Special Report: Trust in the Workplace*. Retrieved from https://www.edelman.com/trust/2022-trust-barometer-special-report-trust-workplace*

*Gallup. (2020). *Employee Burnout: Causes and Cures*. Retrieved from https://www.gallup.com/workplace/237059/employee-burnout-part-main-causes.aspx*

*Goleman, D. (1995). *Emotional Intelligence: Why It Can Matter More Than IQ*. Bantam Books.*

*Levitin, D. J. (2014). *The Organized Mind: Thinking Straight in the Age of Information Overload*. Dutton.*

*Maxwell, J. C. (2007). *The Maxwell Daily Reader: 365 Days of Insight to Develop the Leader Within You and Influence Those Around You*. Thomas Nelson.*

*Porter, M. E., & Nohria, N. (2018). How CEOs Manage Time. *Harvard Business Review, 96*(4), 42-51.*

*Roosevelt, T. (1910). *Citizenship in a Republic*, speech delivered at the Sorbonne, Paris, April 23, 1910.*

*Sinek, S. (2014). *Leaders Eat Last: Why Some Teams Pull Together and Others Don't*. Portfolio.*

*Thurman, H. (2006). *The Living Wisdom of Howard Thurman: A Visionary for Our Time* (W. E. Fluker, Ed.). Skinner House Books.*

Made in the USA
Columbia, SC
23 June 2025

59741403R00065